MATH IN OUR WORLD

MEASURING
ON A TREASURE HUNT

By Jennifer Marrewa
Photographs by Kay McKinley

Reading consultant: Susan Nations, M.Ed.,
author/literacy coach/consultant in literacy development
Math consultant: Rhea Stewart, M.A., mathematics content specialist

WEEKLY READER®
PUBLISHING

Please visit our web site at **www.garethstevens.com**
For a free color catalog describing our list of high-quality books,
call 1-800-542-2595 (USA) or 1-800-387-3178 (Canada). Our fax: 1-877-542-2596

Library of Congress Cataloging-in-Publication Data

Marrewa, Jennifer.
    Measuring on a treasure hunt / Jennifer Marrewa.
        p. cm. — (Math in our world. Level 2)
     ISBN-13: 978-0-8368-9007-5 (lib. bdg.)
     ISBN-10: 0-8368-9007-8 (lib. bdg.)
     ISBN-13: 978-0-8368-9016-7 (softcover)
     ISBN-10: 0-8368-9016-7 (softcover)
    1. Measurement—Juvenile literature. I. Title.
    QA465.M38   2008
    516'.15—dc22   2007033381

This edition first published in 2008 by
Weekly Reader® Books
An Imprint of Gareth Stevens Publishing
1 Reader's Digest Road
Pleasantville, NY 10570-7000 USA

Senior Editor: Brian Fitzgerald
Creative Director: Lisa Donovan
Graphic Designer: Alexandria Davis

Printed in the United States

1 2 3 4 5 6 7 8 9 10 09 08 07

TABLE OF CONTENTS

Words that appear in the glossary are printed in
boldface type the first time they occur in the text.

Chapter 1:
Surprise!

Mrs. Perez has a surprise for the class today. The children gather on the rug. Karley notices a large sheet of paper taped to the blackboard. The paper says, "Clue One." What could this mean? Karley raises her hand to ask Mrs. Perez.

Mrs. Perez says that she has hidden a treasure in the room. She has written and hidden **clues,** too. The clues will lead students to the treasure. Mrs. Perez asks Monica to take the clue off the board. Monica reads it aloud.

The clue says, "Go to a quiet place. Then walk 10 heel-to-toe steps toward the windows and look down." Mrs. Perez asks Jeremy to follow the directions. He goes to the Reading Center. Then he walks 10 steps toward the windows. He looks down. He sees the next clue.

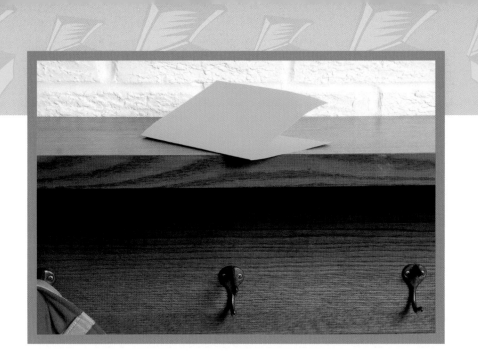

Jeremy opens the clue. Inside is a shoelace. The clue says, "Walk the **length** of 9 shoelaces. Go toward a place with things that keep you warm." Coats keep you warm!

Mrs. Perez asks Andy to follow the directions. Andy walks toward the coats. There he finds the third clue.

Mrs. Perez asks Kelly to read the third clue aloud. The clue says, "Go the length of 15 chairs toward the leader's spot." Mrs. Perez is the leader! She asks Chris to follow the directions. Chris takes 15 steps toward Mrs. Perez's desk. He ends up at the front row of desks.

Mrs. Perez asks Anne to help Chris. Anne spots a box on one of the chairs. The clue says, "Treasure." She carries the box to the rug. Mrs. Perez asks Anne to give the box to Steven. Steven opens the box and finds a surprise for everyone. Pencils are inside!

Chapter 2:
Planning a Treasure Hunt

Now Mrs. Perez wants the students to plan treasure hunts of their own. She splits the class into two groups. The groups will plan treasure hunts for each other. They will write clues. They will hide treasures. It will take a lot of planning.

One group will plan a treasure hunt outside. The other group will plan a treasure hunt inside. Both groups need to use measurement in their clues. They will look for objects and think of ideas.

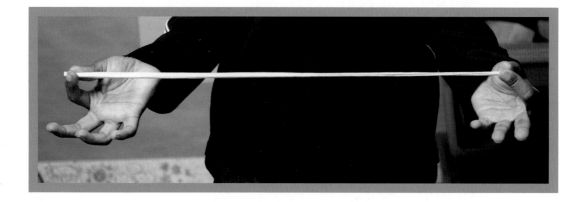

One group goes outside with Mrs. Perez to look for a place to hide their treasure. Andy has some string. The group thinks they can use the string to **measure.** They will use string lengths for one of the clues. They also will use heel-to-toe steps to measure.

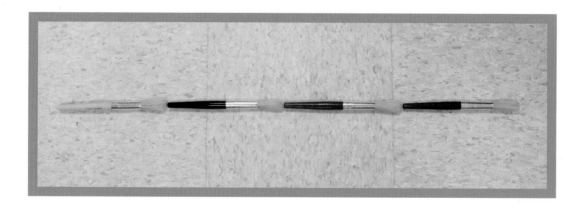

The other group goes with the art teacher. They go to the art room. The group plans to hide their treasure there. Monica thinks they can use the length of a paintbrush to measure. They can use floor tiles to measure, too. They start to measure so they can write the clues.

The group outside plans the spot for their treasure first. Then they write clues. The group in the art room makes a list of clues first. Then they use the clues to pick a place for the treasure.

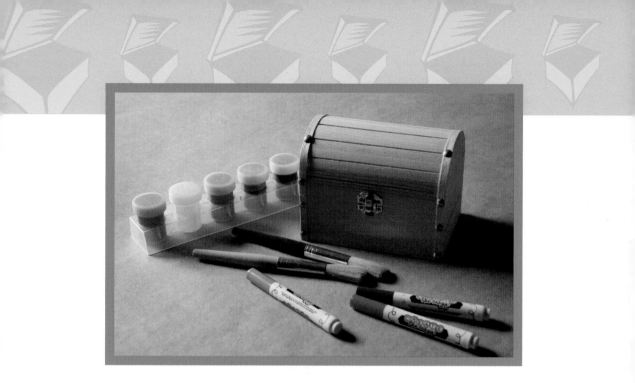

Mrs. Perez collects the clues from each group. She gives each group a box to decorate. Each group will bring treasures from home.

The groups will hide treasures in the boxes before the hunt tomorrow. The boxes will have something for everyone.

Chapter 3:
The Outdoor Treasure Hunt

The treasure hunts are today! The first group heads outside. They hide their clues and the treasure. They do not hide the first clue. They will hand this clue to the other group. The students are excited.

The outdoor treasure hunt begins! The students read the first clue. The clue says, "Go to a place where you can get a drink. Then walk 10 heel-to-toe steps toward a grassy place." A water fountain is a good place to get a drink!

The group walks to the fountain. Tanya takes 10 heel-to-toe steps toward the grassy field. She finds another clue. She sees a string with this clue. The clue says, "Walk the length of 14 strings. Go toward a fun place." The playground is a fun place!

Kayla walks the length of 14 strings toward the playground. There she finds another clue. A jump rope is with this clue. The clue says, "Go toward a shady spot. Walk the length of 3 jump ropes." The students follow the clue, and they find the treasure!

Chapter 4:
The Indoor Treasure Hunt

Now it is time for the indoor treasure hunt. The class goes to the art room. The group reads the first clue. The clue says, "Go to the place where paper, paints, and brushes are stored. Then walk toward tall objects. Walk the length of 11 paintbrushes." They go to the paints and brushes.

The students get a paintbrush from the shelf. Sabine measures the length of 11 paintbrushes toward tall **easels**. She finds a clue there. This clue says, "Go 16 floor tiles. Go toward a colorful place." The art wall where student paintings are displayed is full of colors.

Britt walks 16 floor tiles. She finds the third clue. The clue says, "Go toward the place where light comes in. Go the length of 9 pencil boxes." The students follow the directions. They walk toward the windows. Mike sees a bright box. It is the treasure!

Both groups return to class with their treasures. They talk about the clues they found. They also talk about the different objects they used to measure.

Everyone in the class had a great time. The treasure hunts were so much fun!

Glossary

clue: a hint that helps solve a problem. The hint may be words or pictures.

easel: a stand used for holding a picture

length: the measure of something from end to end

measure: to use units to find the size or length of something

About the Author

Jennifer Marrewa is a former elementary school teacher who writes children's books, poetry, nonfiction, and supplemental learning materials. She lives in California with her husband and two young children.